MANY MONSTERS CAN BLOW FLAMES OUT OF THEIR NOSE

MONSTER SKIN is scaly, slimy, hairy, or all of the above.

VERY HANDY FOR LIGHTING THE GRILL.

MONSTERS HAVE BAD BREATH!

PU!

Everything I Know About
MONSTERS

A collection of made-up facts,
educated Guesses and silly pictures
about CREATURES of CREEPINESS

by TOM LICHTENHELD

SIMON AND SCHUSTER

London   New York   Sydney

MONSTER TRACKS

(ice cream drips)

I'M NO MONSTEROLOGIST, but I do know enough about monsters to draw some pictures. And I can make up more stuff, so I can draw more pictures.

The most important thing I know about monsters is that there really are no such things! No monsters, ever, nowhere, no-how.

In fact, there are no proven cases of any child ever being pinched, grabbed, tickled, slobbered upon or devoured whole by an actual monster.

But, monsters DO exist in our imaginations. And, as you know, our imaginations are immensely HUGE. (Your imagination is so huge that sometimes it leaks out of your ears as earwax.) So, there are lots of monsters and lots of stories about monsters. And, since I've been accused of being one of the best story-maker-uppers ever,* I am going to tell you Everything I Know About Monsters.

* by my mum.

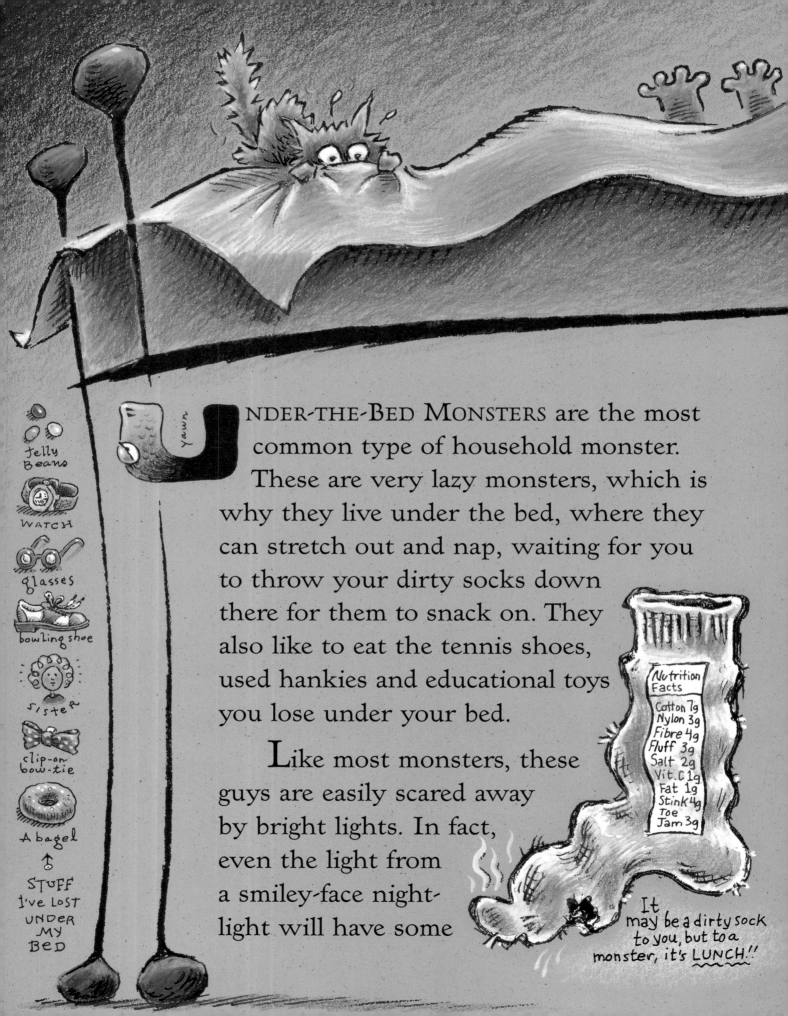

Jelly Beans

WATCH

glasses

bowling shoe

sister

clip-on bow-tie

A bagel
↑
STUFF
I've LOST
UNDER
MY
BED

yawn

UNDER-THE-BED MONSTERS are the most common type of household monster. These are very lazy monsters, which is why they live under the bed, where they can stretch out and nap, waiting for you to throw your dirty socks down there for them to snack on. They also like to eat the tennis shoes, used hankies and educational toys you lose under your bed.

Like most monsters, these guys are easily scared away by bright lights. In fact, even the light from a smiley-face night-light will have some

Nutrition Facts

Cotton 7g
Nylon 3g
Fibre 4g
Fluff 3g
Salt 2g
Vit.C 1g
Fat 1g
Stink 4g
Toe Jam 3g

It may be a dirty sock to you, but to a monster, it's LUNCH.!!

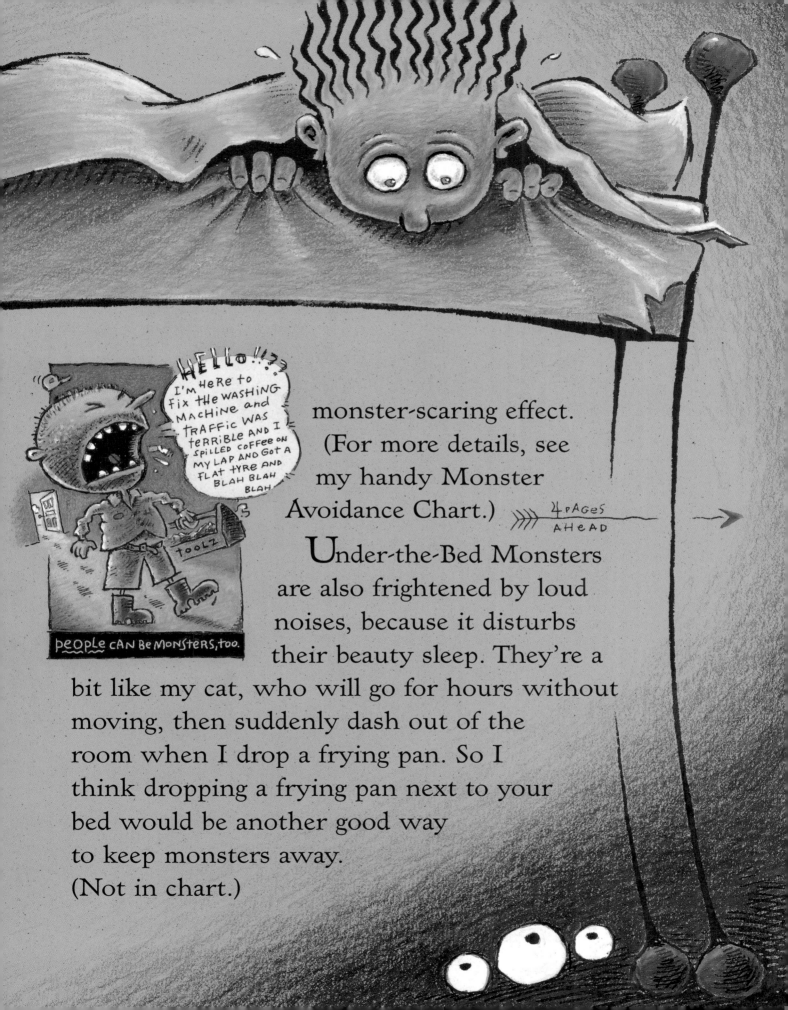

HELLO!!!?? I'M HERE to fix tHe WASHiNG MaChiNe and TRaFFiC WAS terrible AND I SPilLED coFfee oN MY LAP AND Got A FLAt tYRe aNd BLAH BLAH BLAH

PEOPLE CAN BE MONSTERS, too.

monster-scaring effect. (For more details, see my handy Monster Avoidance Chart.) 4 PAGES AHEAD

Under-the-Bed Monsters are also frightened by loud noises, because it disturbs their beauty sleep. They're a bit like my cat, who will go for hours without moving, then suddenly dash out of the room when I drop a frying pan. So I think dropping a frying pan next to your bed would be another good way to keep monsters away. (Not in chart.)

THE MOST COMMON type of Under-the-Bed Monster is the Triple-Tentacled Tickler. Every part of the Triple-Tentacled Tickler is made for tickling, from their long wiggly toes to their waggly ears. They have buck teeth and are made of raspberry jelly.

Here's how to tell if one of these pesky varmints is hiding under your bed. **1.** You hear buck-toothed giggling. **2.** You had vanilla ice cream for dessert, but there's definitely a strong smell of raspberry jelly.

Even Monsters like Birthdays!

the TRIPLE-TENTACLED TICKLER

BUNK-BED MONSTERS are smaller than normal under-the-bed monsters so that two of them can fit under the bed when you sleep over at your friend's house. They're more likely to keep you awake all night with their petty bickering and fighting than by  tickling or grabbing you.

Speaking of sleep-overs, have you ever noticed how your friend's house always smells different and kind of weird? That's actually the smell of their monsters, which you're not used to.

EVERYBODY'S MONSTERS SMELL DIFFERENT.

CUPBOARD MONSTERS live in your cupboard (duh!), and spend all night trying on your clothes.

Because they're bigger than you and have extra arms and legs, they stretch out your shirts, rip big holes in the knees of your jeans, and poke claw-holes in your shoes. When they're finished, they just throw everything on the floor and never hang up your clothes properly the way you always do.

Some cupboard monsters will also chew on your toys.

YUM!
CRUNCH!

Fortunately, Cupboard Monsters usually* disappear when you open the door, but you have to move all the junk at the back of your cupboard, because it's still dark back there and you have to leak in some monster-proofing light to scare them away.

*This will make sense when you see the chart—honest.

YOUNG MAN, WHAT ON EARTH HAPPENED TO THIS CUPBOARD?! IT LOOKS LIKE IT'S BEEN ATTACKED BY MONSTERS!!

You're tellin' ME!

How to tell when Mum is upset with you (A Bonus Lesson): Ⓐ Hands on Hips Ⓑ Formal Greetings Ⓒ Exaggerated Context

How much Light does it take?

USE THIS HANDY 💡 Monster Avoidance Chart

Level One ①

Bedroom door open "Just a crack"

Monsters don't like to see this because, besides providing light (EEK!), it also gives you an ESCAPE ROUTE.

Level Two

Night-Lights

Monsters HATE these, especially the ones with smiley faces OR unicorns. Combinations of smiley faces, rainbows, and unicorns are actually considered cruelty to monsters.

BASEMENT MONSTERS come in three types. The Sock Suckers like to eat damp socks (one from every pair), fresh from the dryer. The Ankle Fiend likes socks too, but prefers them stinky, so he grabs yours right off your feet as you walk down the stairs.

Meanwhile, the Tool Ghoul is over in the workshop, turning perfectly good wood into useless junk and mixing up Dad's tools.

Not to worry, though; making these creeps of the deep disappear is child's play. Just stand at the top of the stairs, bang some pots and pans together really

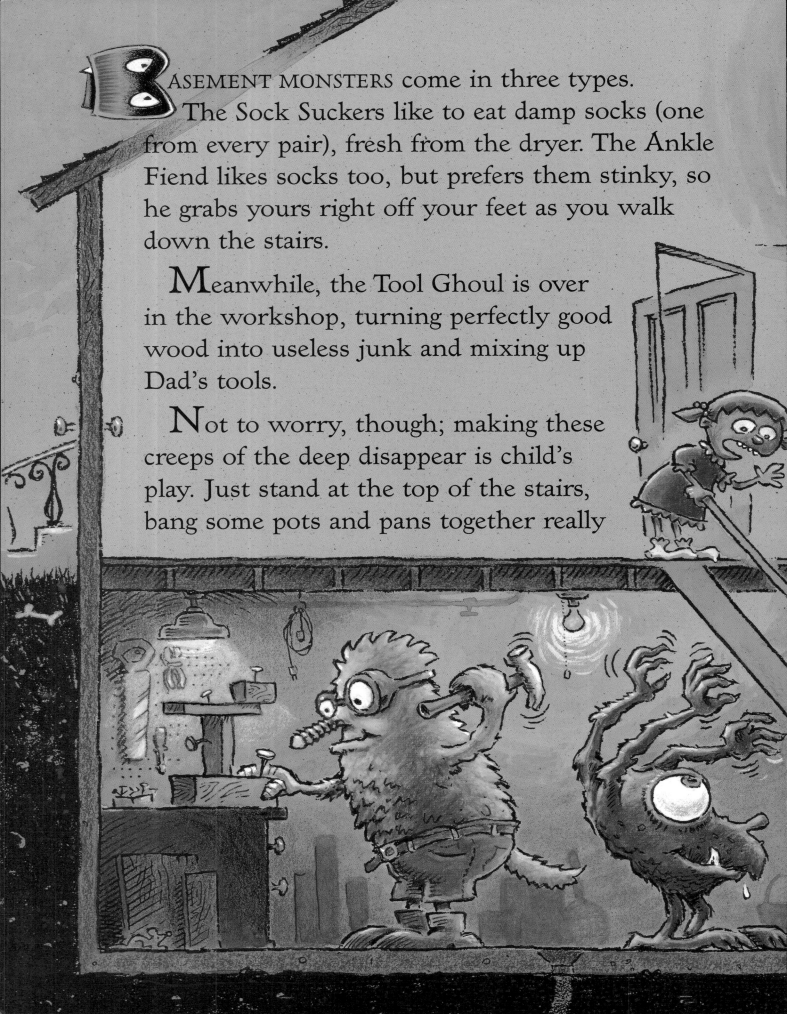

hard and yell down the stairs as loud as you can.

Attic Monsters are the brainiest creatures in the house (except for you), because they sit around all day reading old *National Geographic* magazines that your parents are saving for no apparent reason.

MANY-MOUTHED MIDNIGHT MUNCHER

MONSTERS ARE VORACIOUS EATERS and we're not talking health food here. Other than dirty socks, monsters love anything that's sugar-coated, chocolate-frosted, jelly-glazed, creme-filled, or coconut-covered. And they really like that squirty cream in the spray can.

Monster Food Pyramid*

SUGARY JUNK

SALTY JUNK

DIRTY SOCKS

WAX LIPS

fruit, vegetables, meat loaf, oat bran, tofu

This poor diet is why most monsters are chubby and have awful complexions and bad breath.

Typically, a monster will sneak into your kitchen late at night and eat all the stuff that was meant for your school lunch. Then he'll retire, all bloated and gassy, to his hiding place under your bed. Pretty soon he'll wake up with a tummy ache and need somebody to burp him.

So, the next time you hear moaning from under your bed in the middle of the night, get up and start jumping on the bed. Your monster will feel better for it.

* Built thousands of years ago by Egyptian monsters.

BURP!

AAAAH! THANK YOU!

PFt!

the MOONSTER

SHADOWS are good at pretending to be monsters. Trees, for example, will make shadow monsters at night because they're bored being outside by themselves. But they're totally harmless. Think about it. Shadows can't bite you or grab your ankle or anything. And, if they start to bug you too much, you can get rid of them by just turning on a light. *Poof!* Adios, Mister Shadow Monster!

If you DO see a MONSTER, DON't overReact. It ONLY ENCOURAGES THEM.

DO-it-YOURSELF **MONSTER**

INSTRUCTIONS

1. Get a torch — the BIG oNE!
2. Turn off all the lights in the House.
3. Put torch under your chin and SHiNE it up YouR NoSE.
4. Stomp around the House, growling.

Your very own shadow will sometimes pretend it's a monster and try to sneak up on you. This might happen if it gets tired of following you around all day, or if the pavement is too hot. Of course, as soon as you turn around, it will quickly lie back down and act as if nothing has happened.

Shadow MoNSteR acting innocent.

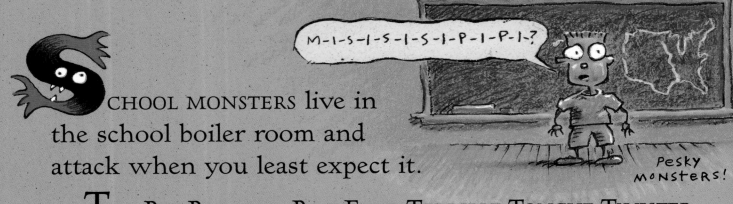

SCHOOL MONSTERS live in the school boiler room and attack when you least expect it.

PESKY MONSTERS!

THE BIG BUMMED BUG EYED TERRIBLE TONGUE TWISTER sneaks up on you when you're at the front of the class, grabs the words as they come out of your mouth and turns them into nonsense. This makes it difficult for your classmates to see you as the genius that you are.

The B.B.B.E.T.T.T. will also attack your parents, which explains why their lectures sound like this: "Youmgxalgorgstopgafbxthatpfbonkrightsnfxlnow!!"

THE HOMEWORK HASHER attacks in the middle of the night, after your homework is done and neatly put away. He eats your homework or erases everything, making it look like you didn't even do it at all. Needless to say, parents and teachers don't believe in the existence of the Hasher.

YUM! GRADE A!

the Homework Hasher

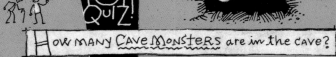

Hey, POP it's for you.

POP QUIZ!

HOW MANY CAVE MONSTERS are in the cave?

A: One. Cave monsters have six eyes.

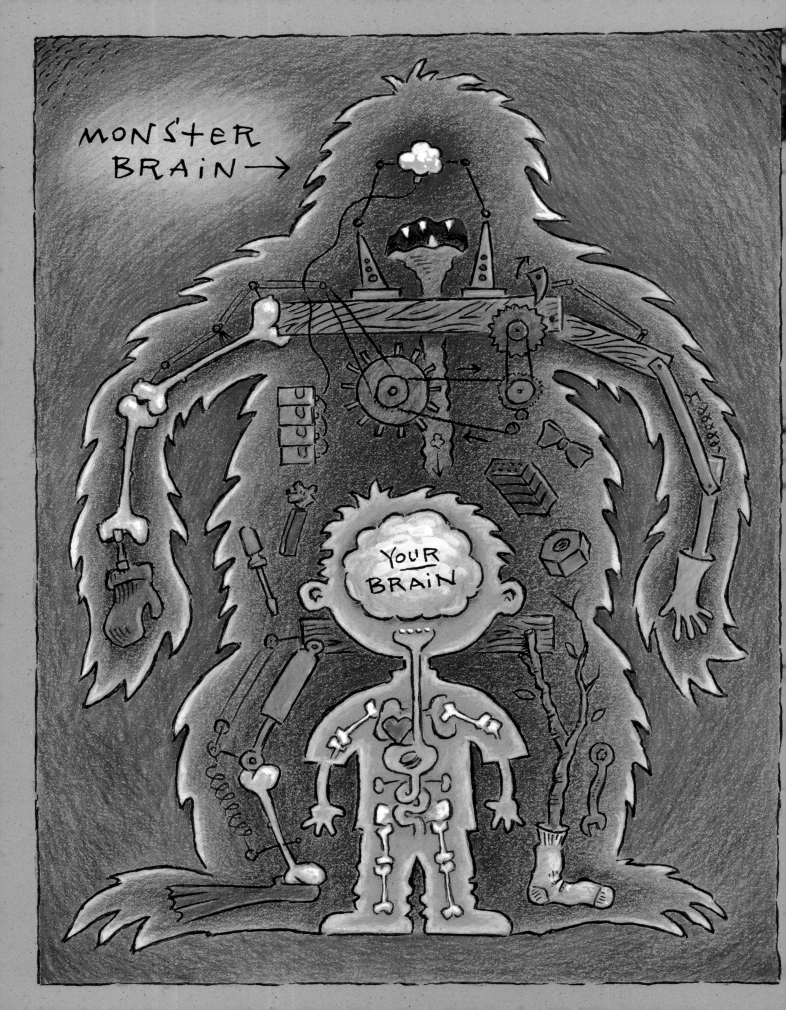

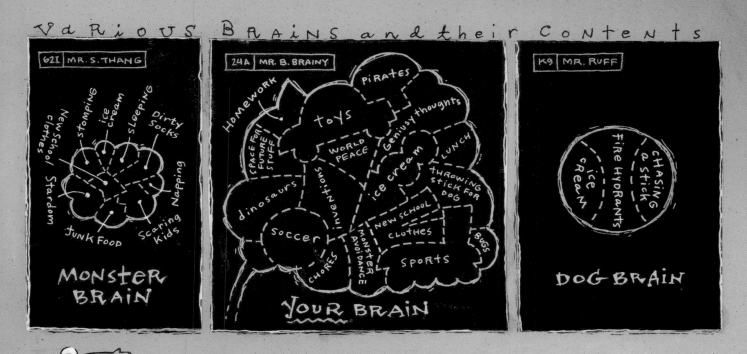

MONSTER BRAIN — 621 MR. S. THANG
(labels: New School clothes, Stomping, ice cream, Sleeping, Dirty Socks, Stardom, Napping, Junk Food, Scaring Kids)

YOUR BRAIN — 24A MR. B. BRAINY
(labels: Homework, Pirates, toys, Geniusy thoughts, Space for future stuff, WORLD PEACE, ice cream, LUNCH, dinosaurs, inventions, Throwing stick for dog, soccer, Monster Avoidance, New School clothes, Bugs, chores, Sports)

DOG BRAIN — K9 MR. RUFF
(labels: CHASING a stick, Fire HydRaNts, ice cream)

EVEN THOUGH monsters are usually bigger than you, their brains are always smaller than yours. And, as you can see in this scientific diagram, monster brains are filled with useless junk, while your brain is packed with important, brainiac stuff. So you can always outwit a monster.

However, you have to watch out for monsters because they're so stupid. For instance, if you took a monster to the shopping centre, he would probably eat the whole jelly bean stall, including the jelly bean stall lady. That's how stupid monsters are.

Also notice that dogs are too clever to worry about monsters.

← (The DOG is included just because he got in the way when the X-ray was taken.)

YUM!

EEK!

A MoNSteR at the SHOPPing centre

DOG BRAIN

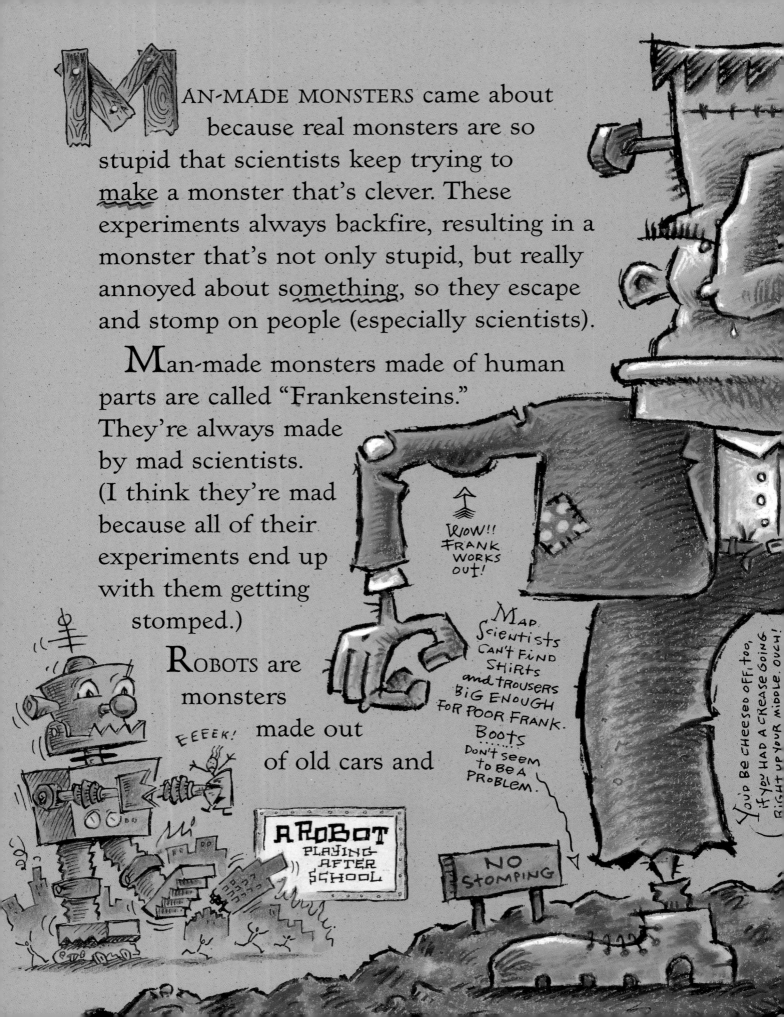

MAN-MADE MONSTERS came about because real monsters are so stupid that scientists keep trying to <u>make</u> a monster that's clever. These experiments always backfire, resulting in a monster that's not only stupid, but really annoyed about <u>something</u>, so they escape and stomp on people (especially scientists).

Man-made monsters made of human parts are called "Frankensteins." They're always made by mad scientists. (I think they're mad because all of their experiments end up with them getting stomped.)

ROBOTS are monsters made out of old cars and

WOW!! FRANK WORKS OUT!

MAD SCIENTISTS CAN'T FIND SHIRTS and TROUSERS BIG ENOUGH FOR POOR FRANK. BOOTS DON'T SEEM TO BE A PROBLEM.

You'D BE CHEESED OFF, too, if you had a crease GOING RIGHT UP YOUR MIDDLE. OUCH!

EEEEK!

A ROBOT PLAYING AFTER SCHOOL

NO STOMPING

toasters. They're miracles of modern science, capable of performing complex tasks with precision and efficiency, until they go haywire. Then they, too, just want to stomp on things.

Robots aren't much fun because they don't scream, stink, get bug-eyed, or have out-of-control body fluids.

TV and MOVIE MONSTERS

Lots of monsters audition for parts in monster movies, but they never get the parts because they're such lousy actors. They don't follow directions well, they forget what they're supposed to say and they run away whenever those big movie lights come on. So, movie monsters are played by humans wearing big monster costumes. (Next time you're watching a monster

Just some guy →

MOVIE MONSTER (FRONT VIEW)

MOVIE MONSTER (BACK VIEW)

Pete

I HAVE a PEDICURE IN aN HOUR.

Harry

CASTING DEPT.

NEXT!

movie, walk right up to the screen and you'll be able to
see the zips on their costumes.)

It's easy being a movie monster
because the scripts are always the
same. They usually go like this:
First, somebody criticises a
monster for being (a) ugly, (b) dopey,
or (c) stinky. This makes the monster

NO! NO! You SILLY
MONSTER! YOU'RE NOT
SUPPOSED TO EAT WITH
THE CHILDREN, YOU'RE
SUPPOSED TO EAT
THE CHILDREN!

But I like
peanut butter
way better.

WHY MONSTERS MAKE LOUSY ACTORS

angry, so he stomps on the critical person, a few tall
buildings and a city bus. Finally, the army saves the day
with bazookas, flame-throwers, and dive-bombers. (Oh
yes, somewhere in there a pretty girl gets a crush on
the monster despite his being ugly, dopey and stinky.)

AFTER A RAINSTORM, THE PUDDLEMONSTERS COME OUT

ALIENS FROM OUTER SPACE aren't officially part of the monster kingdom, but they are really fun to draw and you get to give them cool names like "Belchblasters."

Aliens always land their spaceships in the desert where people have put out big signs that say Free Parking for Aliens! Then they roam around looking for some humans so they can take over their brains.

Having your brain taken over by aliens isn't as bad as it sounds because it gives you an excuse to do stupid things like lose your homework or punch your brother for no reason or watch cartoons on TV when it's perfectly gorgeous outside.

After buying some earth souvenirs at Ye Olde Earth Gift Shoppe, aliens head back to their own planet. The next day they go to school and write a report called, "How I took over Bobby Yablonski's brain and all the stupid things I made him do."

GOLLY MUM, THIS TUNA CASSEROLE IS AWESOME! WHEN CAN WE HAVE LIVER?

NO HAT

HAIR COMBED

EARS CLEAN

NOT PLAYING WITH FOOD

PEOPLE WHO'VE HAD THEIR BRAINS TAKEN OVER BY ALIENS ACT VERY STRANGELY.

DOGS LOVE FLYING SAUCERS.

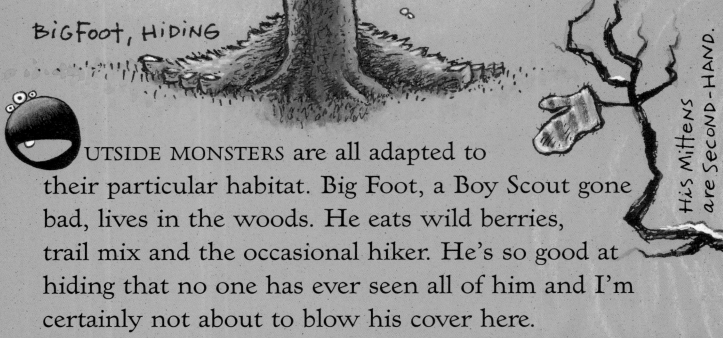
BiGFooT, HiDiNG

His Mittens are Second-hand.

OUTSIDE MONSTERS are all adapted to their particular habitat. Big Foot, a Boy Scout gone bad, lives in the woods. He eats wild berries, trail mix and the occasional hiker. He's so good at hiding that no one has ever seen all of him and I'm certainly not about to blow his cover here.

THE "SWAMP THANG" is sort of a part-fish, part-toady creature who lives in mucky goop. He's been the subject of lots of monster movies

OUTHOUSE MONSTER (2-HOLER)

because his big flipper feet are excellent for stomping. Whatever you do, don't play with his beach toys or call him "Fish Lips."

"Swamp Thang"
ONE SLIMY DUDE

WHO BURST MY BEACH BALL?

OUTHOUSE MONSTERS are actually toilet monsters who've gone "back to nature." They're low-down bum-biters and number one at living in number two.

THOSE ARE ALL THE MONSTERS I can think of, but I'll bet you can come up with loads more. If you need a little help, use my patented Monster Maker to give your imagination a kick start.

Then, your monsters and my monsters can get together at the Annual Monster Reunion Picnic. This is where all kinds of monsters get together and play games, have kid-scaring contests and

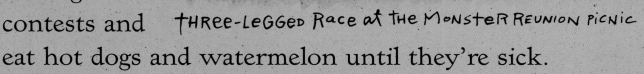

THREE-LEGGED RACE at the MONSTER REUNION PICNIC

eat hot dogs and watermelon until they're sick.

Then they all go home for another year of tickling, tormenting, stomping, chomping, sock-eating, bum-biting, belch-blasting, underwear-tearing and whatever else you and your monstrous imagination can come up with.

Meeting the Relatives at the REUNION PICNIC.

HI. I'M YOUR ANT.

the end

SIMON AND SCHUSTER
First published in the UK by Simon & Schuster UK Ltd,
Africa House, 64-78 Kingsway, London WC2B 6AH.

Originally published by Simon and Schuster Books for Young Readers,
an imprint of Simon and Schuster Children's Publishing Division,
1230 Avenue of the Americas, New York, New York 10020.

A CIP catalogue record for this book is available from the
British Library upon request.

Book design by Tom Lichtenheld.
The text for this book is set in Hadriano.

The illustrations are rendered in ink, coloured pencil,
crayon, gouache watercolour and raspberry PEZ˚.

ISBN: 0-689-86123-0

Printed in China
2 4 6 8 10 9 7 5 3

TO JAN, WITH LOVE & GRATITUDE

Never let a MONSTER BORROW YOUR sports CAR !

A MONSTER, CAMPING

A MONSTER DRESSED UP FOR HALLOWEEN

BOSS MONSTER

Movie Script
"MONSTER RATS FROM MARS"
MONSTER RATS: GROWL AND STOMP ON THINGS.
KIDS: SCREAM REALLY LOUD WHILE RUNNING EVERY WHICH WAY.
The End

HA HA HA HA HA
LAUGH MONSTER →

THE GRUMPY DAD MONSTER
tell him to:
① TAKE A NAP
② GO BE A PIRATE!

LOCHNESS MONSTER (WINTER)